Snakes in the Swamp

I0456217

Commentary on the First 100 Days

By Don Storch

Books by Don Storch

Snakes in the Swamp

If a Passive-Progressive Leads from behind he
is a Double Oxymoron

ISBN:1547074671
ISBN:9781547074679

Dedication

**This book is dedicated to my wife and Muse
Jeanne Klier Storch**

"Well begun is half done."
Aristotle

Prologue

'Snakes in the Swamp' come in the form of bureaucrats, Republicans, Democrats, spies in the form of the FBI, CIA, NSA, lobbyists, consultants, friends, politicians – who make for strange bedfellows – and any other varmint living within the metropolitan radius of Washington DC., such as the Media. Not all are reptiles, but there are enough from within to turn a non-politician, businessman into 'Crocodile Dundee.'

Donald J. Trump a billionaire real estate mogul from New York, who never ran for public office, entered the 2016 Republican primaries for President of the United States against 16 others, mostly Republican elitist operatives, beat the field in the primaries and then faced the favorite Democratic nominee, Hillary Clinton, a polished left wing progressive politician who knew how to skirt the law; nevertheless, against all odds, the Donald defied pollsters, political pundits, the left wing progressive main stream media and a rigged political system to become President of the United States.

Trump used a not so secret weapon, first ever employed by a presidential candidate – a Tweet with only 140 characters. He tweeted every morning taking his messages directly to the public, bypassing the media he didn't like, trust, and from his perspective delivered fake news.

President Trump filled the vacuum left by his predecessor President Barack Hussein Obama, who failed the middle class with empty promises, serving up a black community organizer in himself, a silver tongue orator who delivered eight years of Alinsky philosophy, socialist programs, duplicitous messages, hypocritical policies, both domestic and foreign, and mendacious rhetoric, all of which created divisiveness and racism that failed to unite the people and set America back a decade.

Trump's opponent, Hillary Clinton, who served under Obama as Secretary of State, promised more of the same.

The public had enough of the joblessness, the stalled economy, the stagnant wages, the failed domestic and foreign policies, the racism and the terrorism threatened by radical Islamic Terrorists called ISIS, who President Obama refused to recognize.

Trump came along at the right time with the right message, even if it was Tweeted.

"Snakes in the Swamp" is a collection of commentary on the first 100 days of President Trump.

Fake News

Fake news has been around since humans have been communicating with each other. Although President Trump didn't discover it, he has certainly brought attention to it and rightly so. Fake news comes in many forms, from many sources and is disseminated by news outlets, some even considered to be credible. Some fake news is downright false, other forms of fake news can come about through innuendo, implication or by the way in which a writer strings a story together, even with facts.

The next closest thing to fake news is negative news with bias. Trump has been the victim of both. Trump calls it a "Witch Hunt," which it appears to be. Negative news with intent and in collusion with one party, in this case the Democratic Party, is a conspiracy which is what is taking place in the United States and can erode a democracy.

Trump has made this charge and a recent study at Harvard University confirmed it.

No politician in history has been treated worse or more unfairly by the media than Trump.

The report, based on an analysis of news reports in the print editions of The New York Times, The Wall Street Journal, and The Washington Post, the main newscasts of CBS, CNN, Fox News, and NBC, and three European news outlets (The UK's Financial Times and BBC, and Germany's ARD), found that media coverage of Trump's first 100 days set a new standard for negativity at 80 percent negative coverage.

For comparison sake, Bill Clinton received 60 percent negative coverage during his first 100 days, George W. Bush had 57 percent and Obama had just 41 percent negative coverage.

In no week did Trump's coverage drop below 70 percent and it reached a 90 percent negative at its peak.

These numbers are appalling and a pox on the house of journalism.

There's an old story about Moses saving his people from the Egyptians by parting the Red Sea.

Moses was leading the Israelites away from the Egyptian Army who were chasing them toward the Red Sea and as they got closer, with their swords flashing in the sunlight, Moshe, Moses public relations person, ran to the front of the column and asked Moses what he was going to do when he got to the Red Sea.

Moses looked at the young flak and said, 'Son when I get to the sea I will part the waters by spreading my arms like this, and allow my people to safely reach the other side. Then, I will allow the Egyptians to get to the middle of the sea and I will close my arms like this drowning the enemy.'

Moshe looked up at Moses and said, 'Do it like you say, and I'll get you 10 pages in the Old Testament.'

Merriam-Webster defines fake as a thing that is not genuine or, what is not what it purports to be.

In the early days of Catholicism, they called it propaganda and Merriam-Webster defines it as spreading of ideas, information, or rumor for helping or injuring an institution, a cause, or a person.

As President Trump looked down from the podium from the Capitol steps to the Washington Monument delivering his inaugural address he saw the crowds and thought these must be greater than what President Obama got during his first inaugural address, despite the inclement weather.

Little did Trump know there was an editor out there that assigned a photographer to take a picture from the top of the Washington Monument back to the Capital. When the photographer got to the Washington Monument he found the elevator to the top was out of order.

He climbed some 899 steps to the top and took the picture. Back in the newsroom the editor who assigned the photo with devious intent had a similar picture of the Obama inauguration and when comparing the two there appeared to be more people at the Obama inauguration.

The two photos were published side-by-side and Trump subsequently made an issue of the two photos calling it 'fake' news and claiming his crowd was larger than Obama's.

During the second week, the Prime Minister of the UK, Theresa May visited with Trump. There was a photo op in the Oval Office and May and Trump were photographed standing on either side of a bust of Winston Churchill, which had been removed from the Oval Office by Obama but Trump requested it be placed back in the Oval Office.

A pool reporter from Time Magazine, Zeke Miller, was covering the photo op and looked for the bust of Martin Luther King which was placed in the Oval Office when Obama became president. It was there on that day also but the Time reporter couldn't see it, claiming that a camera man may have been standing in front of it; nevertheless, he Tweeted that Trump had removed the bust. His Tweet hit 3,000 news outlets and it was declared fake news.

Throughout the presidential campaign, and up until election night and into the morning of the next day the liberal media, pundits, pollsters, columnists and the bastion of progressivism, the New York Times and the Washington Post were predicting a Clinton landslide – it was the resurrection of fake news in the 21st Century.

It wasn't until after midnight that the liberal media began to see the shock setting in, Trump was winning Middle America, at one point the futures on the stock market were tanking by 800 points recognizing a predictable Clinton win. By the time the media declared Trump a winner the stock market (Dow) rebounded and opened 300 points up, Trump received 306 Electoral votes, a landslide from the Electoral College perspective, and Clinton won the popular vote by a margin of 2.9 million votes, most of which came from California. The center of the map of the USA was red, the outer edges blue, as was the Democratic Party

The crying began at the Clinton headquarters, the protests followed, the de-legitimizing campaign by the Democrats was launched and war was declared.

The rookie won, the enemy was facing PETSD, Post Electoral Traumatic Stress Disorder.

They scrambled, tried to organize protests with no objective, they were aimless, but financially supported by George Soros, investor, business magnet, philanthropist and supporter of progressive political causes and worth $25.2 Billion.

The opposition forces behind the de-legitimizing campaign are identified as selective elitist Republicans, elitist progressive Democrats, some members of the House, the Senate, organizations such as Planned Parenthood, the left-wing mainstream media and even the Judicial branch of government.

Meanwhile in a world wind of activity in some 21 days Trump addressed the remaking of Obamacare, the reform of the tax code, addressing funding for infrastructure projects, passing new trade deals, finding and preserving jobs, keeping companies in the US, immigration reform and the safety of the citizenry and rebuilding the military.

The lights were on around the clock in the White House, suggesting that the occupant didn't need much sleep while, those that worked for him were on the verge of narcolepsy.

PETSD

The Centers for Disease Control (CDC) is reporting that Post Electoral Traumatic Stress Disorder (PETSD) is rampantly spreading among Democrats across the United States and occurred shortly after Trump was elected president, reaching epidemic proportions.

The source of the disorder the CDC says, was the unexpected loss of Hillary Clinton in the general election which has now been exponentially spread by Democratic leaders in both the House and Senate with negative rhetoric and a campaign to de-legitimize the Trump presidency.

The CDC said symptoms manifest themselves in hissy fits, crying episodes, delusional behavior, tantrums, memory loss and the spreading of fake news.

Sen. Elizabeth Warren (D., MA.) who often believes she is a descendant of a native American Indian tribe, took to the Senate floor just weeks after Trump took office with the purpose of opposing and delaying the nomination of Sen. Jeff Sessions as attorney general.

Warren read a quotation of Coretta Scott King, the late wife of Martin Luther King, that was negative of Sessions, and was silenced by the Chair. She was silenced because Senate rules state that one senator cannot impugn another on the Senate floor.

CDC says the only way of preventing the spread of this disorder is by placing a quarantine over negative rhetoric by Democrats in the House and the Senate, but this would be a violation of the first amendment.

Signs of PETSD surfaced during the Clinton-Trump presidential campaign when Hillary Clinton called Trump supporters, 'deplorables and irredeemables.'

It further surfaced when Senate Minority Leader Chuck Schumer (D., NY) broke down crying over President Trump's executive order to keep America safe by temporarily banning refugees coming into the US from certain countries because there was no way of properly vetting them.

And then at a press conference House Minority Leader Nancy Pelosi (D., Ca.) suffering a senior moment, said, "While it's only been a couple of weeks since the inauguration, we've seen nothing that I can work with President Bush on."

In this incidence, it was not clear whether she was talking about President George W. Bush of eight years ago, or President George H. W. Bush of 24 years ago, but we do know she was talking about President Donald J. Trump of two weeks ago.

And then there was Maxine Waters (D., CA.) who is having trouble representing herself, least of all others, who thinks, "Russia was invading Korea."

The CDC said PETSD can be controlled with counseling, medication and about four years of treatment. However, if the etiology is not removed after this period, the condition becomes chronic.

New World Order

The once Alinsky influenced Chicago community organizer, Barack Hussein Obama, former apologetic progressive President of the United States, is launching a campaign to introduce a new world order which he plans to lead under the auspices of the United Nations.

After he departed his presidency he took a respite with a few rounds of golf in Palm Springs, and then moved on courtesy of Richard Branson's Virgin Airlines, to the British Virgin Islands to enjoy Branson's secluded island enclave where they did some kite surfing together.

Obama's post presidency game plan is to sabotage the presidency of Donald J. Trump and to preserve his own presidential legacy which is in dire trouble because of his own failures of the past eight years, an unprecedented un-American form of activity for a past president.

It is much like playing a bad pro basketball game over the weekend and trying to replay it on Monday to clarify history.

The initiative of battle by Obama is to draw the lines on immigration, Obamacare, race relations and climate change. These issues will change with the times.

It all began following Trump's upset victory, and the revitalization of OFA, the Organizing for Action group Obama formed during his campaign for the presidency which continued to operate during his two terms as president.

Media reports Obama tweeting from OFA accounts giving marching orders to his foot soldiers:

"It is fine for everybody to feel stressed, sad, discouraged," he said in a conference call from the White House. "But get over it." He demanded they "move forward to protect what we've accomplished. Now is the time for some organizing," he said. "So don't mope."

According to Paul Sperry, author of "The Great American Bank Robbery," OFA activists helped organize anti-Trump marches across US cities, some of which turned into riots, after Trump issued a temporary ban on immigration from seven terror-prone Muslim nations.

OFA is run by old Obama aids and campaign workers. Tax records show "nonpartisan' OFA has some 32,525 volunteers nationwide and is registered as a 501 © (4) and doesn't have to disclose its donors. OFA has raised more than $40 million in contributions since evolving from Obama's campaign organization.

Trump Delivers on Promises; Main Stream Media Undermines Them; McCain Criticizes Trump on Foreign Soil

In one month President Trump takes steps to deliver what he promised during his presidential campaign while left wing progressives, still smarting from their loss, attempt to de-legitimize his presidency and the left wing main stream media goes beyond its adversarial role to undermine the positive evolving from the Trump administration.

The Democrats in Congress delay, linger and walk back Trump cabinet appointments and Sen John McCain (R-AZ.) pulls an Obama and criticizes Trump on foreign soil. McCain, one of the elitists Republicans originally opposing Trump's nomination, is too probably smarting over his failed attempts to reach the Oval office.

McCain says in Germany that the Trump administration is in 'disarray' and criticizes Trump for blasting the main stream media over fake news for which it is guilty of publishing from the New York Times to the Washington Post. Both have apologized for it, both have had writers that have written it and only recently the AP moved a story that Trump was going to use the National Guard to round up illegal immigrants. Not true!

McCain defended the press by saying in Germany that an adversarial press is necessary, without it he said it can be the beginning of a dictatorship.

However, the media is so adversarial today that you can't find a positive story on Trump, despite significant accomplishments. The Times is so adversarial it could be considered the leader of the communications arm of the progressive left-wing party among the rest of the main stream media. One month in office and some are questioning editorially whether Trump can finish one term.

The forces against Trump are formidable: from a shadow government being formed by former President Obama and his OFA troops of more than 32,000 nationwide (Organizing for Action) to intelligence bureaucratic moles held over from the Obama administration and Democratic protesters, trained to be safely arrested, with funding by multi-billionaire George Soros; there is a well-oiled protest/riot machine operating that pays little attention to the law.

Nevertheless, Trump has provided Americans with more optimism, hope and promise in one month than Obama ever did for a moment in his eight years.

Quite to the contrary, one more term of Obama and America would have been destroyed.

Trump delivers on his promises: he has already saved more than 200,000 jobs and received pledges from corporations of more than $80 billion in the construction of new facilities in the US.

He has improved economy with records being set in the stock market.

He is in the process of repealing and replacing Obamacare; reducing taxes; providing jobs, addressing immigration, infrastructure and the wall; law enforcement, security for the nation and the build-up of the military with the philosophy of peace through strength.

In a record setting press conference, he told the media, organizations and individuals, what he thought of their fake news and told them he was going to continue to tell them what he thought and call them out on it. And, whenever he can by pass them he will through Twitter and the rally he held thereafter in Marathon Fl. drawing 10,000.

Trump's actions to date appear to be promises and change one can believe in, unlike the elitists politicians from either party of the past.

What People Think

The New York Times thinks it publishes, 'All the News that's fit to Print,' the Washington Post thinks, 'Democracy Dies in Darkness' and journalist Mika Brezeznski of MSNBC thinks, 'Our Job' is to control, 'Exactly what people think.'

And, you really believe that the main stream media doesn't print 'fake news,' or only the news they think you should see?

My Oh My, if that's what the public thinks how gullible they must be — but I know that's not true, or Donald J. Trump wouldn't be President.

And Twitter, wouldn't be able to beat the main stream media daily with the president's posts.

Whoever would have thought Twitter would be a part of the beat of main stream media reporters if they want to cover the president?

The New York Times with its motto apparently prints only what it thinks, is 'fit to print,' so it too is controlling what its readers can read and the Washington Post with its new motto of, 'Democracy Dies in Darkness' is only news when they shine a light on what they perceive it to be?

NBC with the likes of Mika Brzezinski on Morning Joe — that is in Scarborough — is worried that if the economy turns south, Americans may end up trusting Trump over the media.

And apparently, Brzezinski believes it is her 'job' to control 'exactly what people think.,' not the public's, or the president's because they are not capable of identifying what is fake news.

Perhaps this is because the main stream media has been writing for its audience at the level of a 13th grader or less for quite some time.

Since Trump was elected President of the United States there have been 16 fake stories about him or his presidency, and we're amid an epidemic of fake news. Epidemics are usually conveyed by an agent and then it is spread by the source by susceptible hosts.

The Federalists describes it this way, "The 'agent' in this case is hysteria over Trump's presidency, and the "susceptible hosts" are a slipshod, reckless, and breathtakingly gullible media class that spread the hysteria around like—well, like a virus."

And so, it's gotten so bad teachers from elementary school through college are conducting classes to curb the spread of fake and misleading news, rather than journalism correcting its own problem.

One needs to ask oneself is this because journalism now has a cause greater than Truth and may this be progressive liberalism, and if not, what is the cause that Trump's Truth?

Confirmation of a Judge

The sounds of bias and politics ring as true in the Senate Judiciary Committee's process of confirming a judge for the Supreme Court as it does in the writing by the media of a news story.

As much as Judge Neil Gorsuch, the Supreme Court nominee, successfully sidestepped the Democratic Senators questions of conservative party affiliation and to get him to answer questions about politically dynamic issues such as Roe v Wade which could possibly come before him were he confirmed as a Supreme Court Judge, it didn't stop the bias questions from flowing during the past three days with the intent of a 'gotcha.'

Consistently, Gorsuch said "My personal views have nothing to do with being a Judge and being fair." Or, in another way of saying it, he promised to judge the law and not make the law.

He refused to agree or disagree with what has been established as 'precedent' when asked about cases that have been settled, other than to say, 'that is what it is.'

"I refuse to get involved with politics." If I do answer these questions, 'I am sending a signal.' I don't believe the judiciary should be a party of 'judicial judgement.'

While Gorsuch behaves like a Justice being selected from central casting, it cannot be ignored that at times during this process there is an elephant in the room with him and that is President Donald J. Trump who selected him based upon the history of his political leanings, despite his statements that his job as judge 'is not to make law but to interpret law.'

Nevertheless, it would be naive to believe that bias, or politics if you will, is not injected into the process of confirmation or the legal decisions by the judiciary once a Justice is approved.

It may appear to one that it is a strange juxtaposition to compare the confirmation of a supreme court judge to the writing of a news story.

Unfortunately, there is a lot of commonality.

Do you think for one moment a journalist does not have core values as may well be true with a Supreme Court Justice?

When a Judge makes, a decision does one believe those core values do not play a role in his decision in the court of justice?

Likewise, when a journalist writes a story why wouldn't the story be written and presented with his core values just as Justice might be doing the same in deciding?

What was disingenuous in the confirmation process, was to believe that Gorsuch's position as an 'originalist' in the concept of our founders of the constitution, that politics is not intertwined with the judiciary, any more than politics is intertwined with the media in telling a story.

The real question that was asked, 'does justice depend upon who won the last election?'

There is no question the role the Supreme Court plays in politics, if this were not true why would a presidential election be so dependent upon the direction of a country for decades in relationship to progressiveness v conservatism?

After watching some 20 hours of what Gorsuch and family had to endure, and Sen Grassley had to excuse himself from because of his bedtime, I was impressed by Sen. Lindsey Graham's soliloquies.

It was refreshing, humorous, positive for the party and unfortunate he didn't use it while running for the presidency against Trump.

Whatever all of this was about - it wasn't the economy - it was the politics.

Trump Must Overcome Elitists

From the outset, President Donald J. Trump was not a member of the elitists of the Republican Party, he was not a member of the Club, such as being a member of Yale's Skull & Bones secret society.

Nor are many others of the Republican Party's inner circle, although some may be or have been such as the Bush clan and former Secretary of State John Kerry, but others formed their own club, perhaps not as well known – they are all the elitists, or at least they think they are.

The Republican Party much like the Democratic Party is made-up of the good old boys, oh some girls slipped in, but they are not much of a factor yet, nothing like Yale's Skull & Bones.

Much of our society is like that, you will find it in elitists communities, island enclaves, business clicks, just read the obituaries of the wealthy that pass on and it will give you a history of the power brokers of their time.

Trump was never one of them – he was an interloper, of business fortune and success, he didn't pay his dues and work within the system. He never will be one of them, he is a maverick, an outsider, a non-politician playing by his own rules recognizing what the people of the nation want and need to survive.

He is a character out of the norm, brash, entertaining, charismatic, a playboy, a womanizer, married three times, but with a family unparalleled by most.

Nevertheless, he now finds himself the President of the United States and it turns out that his worst enemy is his own party, not that the Democrats are lagging far behind in their own form of negativity and obstruction.

He is much like a salmon swimming upstream waiting to spawn before a Bear gulps him down for dinner.

And if the swamp he entered in DC was not enough, there is that portion of society, three million of them that he didn't sway his way during the election process of the popular vote.

You see, as the astute businessman he is, he won the election by the electoral vote not the popular vote and it shocked the elitists and now they find themselves, among others of the progressive liberals, in the uncomfortable position of having to deal with it – tears and all.

Moreover, the mainstream media, and higher educational institutions were infiltrated over the years with liberal brainwashing to think this was the only course of direction for our society.

President Trump is a refreshing change for this Nation, and just what it needs in these dire times. Trump, during the GOP primaries of the presidential elections defeated 16 members of the elitist Republicans, among them, those that were part of the 'club' and that have held public office; Bush, of the entitled, Cruz, Graham, Kasich, Paul and Rubio and they still participate as part of his opposition.

There are others, McCain and Romney for example, who had their opportunity to run, but failed, and now serve as critical pundits.

Outside of this, there is past President Barack Hussein Obama, who is running a Shadow Government right in DC.

All of this is taking place while President Trump, even while he was President-Elect, and continued as he became president, was keeping corporations in America, providing jobs, improving the economy – stock market up 16 % – providing safety with immigration policies, moving toward the repeal and replacement of Obamacare, a failed health care policy, and bolstering the US Military.

While middle America is moving forward with optimism there is a segment of the Nation moving backward with divisiveness and values of global negativism.

Globalism is a policy tried, but a failed one. America first is a policy initiated and promising without obstruction, yet to be accomplished.

Truth Without Bias Impossible to Tell

It was the Donald, as in President Trump, that drew to the nation's attention 'Fake News' in a 'Tweet' of 140 characters.

There was nothing new in what he said, it wasn't a revelation, but it was coming from the bully pulpit of a presidential candidate, a president-elect and a president, so it was news.

Few of us can disagree that we haven't seen 'Fake News' reported by the media of yesterday, today and won't read or hear more of it tomorrow.

Reporting 'the News' is not complicated. It has always been based upon the simplicity of the tenets of: Who, What, Where, When, Why and sometimes How.

Answer the questions, put it into an interesting narrative with a compelling lead, draw the reader into the story, tell the truth and you have done your job as a journalist.

However, examine that sentence, an 'interesting narrative' a 'compelling lead' and 'draw the reader into the story' and enter the bias of the story teller.

If that's all that was being done today we would be a fortunate nation, but that is not what is being propagated by the left wing progressive media that is the fuel that fires the hatred, hysteria and the untruthful hyperbole of today's news.

Today's media is forgetting its role as a protector of the first amendment, a protector of the constitution, a check and balance to a nation that is tempted by greed, corruption and those that would bring harm to America.

Their role should be higher than the business it represents. Yes, it is a business, and for it to survive it needs to make money. The media has been in trouble financially for some time trying to adjust to the complexities of today's technology. It is not an early adapter, it is slow in adjusting to change as has been witnessed, however, it is making a serious mistake by stepping out of it's true role in reporting the news with truth and limiting its bias.

Bias is part of every story you read, hear or see.

It is influencing your thinking, the politics of the world, the economy, our culture, the relationship of countries and is being directed by the power brokers of the day with a specific intent of controlling the media.

The media should not be playing a role in these politics, one way or the other, they should be reporting the news with as little bias as possible. After all they are an important check and balance of our Democracy under the constitution and they should live-up to that charge.

They need to return to the tenets of good journalism.

It appears that the news media's motives today go beyond the tenets of good journalism, good business and survival and are incorporated into the political direction of a nation, for which they should not have a role in every story and their multi-media presentations.

I recently reviewed a book a friend gave to me many years after I left journalism and joined the corporation as a PR person for the money I couldn't earn as a reporter.

The book was called, "A Treasury of Great Reporting," by Louis L. Snyder and Richard B. Morris first written in 1949 and republished in 1962 by Simon Schuster.

My friend said in a note on the inside cover as he passed the book on to me, "Take this and use it when life in the Crystal Palace gets you down."

The book delivered the writings of Defoe, Dickens and Kipling to Earnest Hemingway, John Gunther, Marguerite Higgins and Quentin Reynolds.

As the book said, it covered a collection of nearly 300 classic examples of 'literature under pressure.'

The stories ranged in time from the report of a witch's trial and conviction in 1587 to the 1961 trial of Adolf Eichmann.

It would be worth the time of the power brokers of journalism today to review this book and see what journalism once was, and should be again.

Common Sense v No Sense

Political Correctness has seriously invaded the brains of some persons with no sense v common sense in the United States.

In my opinion the cause of a lack of common sense is the influence of left wing progressive liberalism.

It is a serious condition and one day will very likely be diagnosed by the medical community as a condition in need of treatment.

Influencing senseless political correctness often comes about, in my opinion, through an old technique of brain washing. Its origin most likely is Asian, where brain washing was practiced in World War II, Korea and Vietnam

It has become more sophisticated in recent years as it is practiced in the United States by infiltrating the educational system, as is also practiced in China, Russia, Iran, North Korea and elsewhere.

Hopefully the condition, created by progressive left-wing liberals, will be covered by some affordable health care act like Obamacare which is in the process of imploding, if not exploding.

Otherwise it will be a boon for ambulance chasing lawyers until such time laws favor illegal aliens living in all cities in the US rather than just a few to commit heinous crimes, including murder.

Examples of no sense through political correctness can be seen in Rockville MD. where two adults, but illegal aliens, 17 and 18 raped a 14 year-old-child in Rockville, MD. High School, a city seeking to be a sanctuary one. The accused, one from El Salvador and the other from Guatemala, were before the court system in a pending "alien removal case."

The case raises common sense questions such as: Why are illegal aliens allowed to attend public schools? Were these students vetted before being allowed to attend? Do these students have criminal records in their home countries? And why would a school system allow 17 and 18-year-old's to be in the 9th grade when they should be out of high school?

And, in nearby Alexandria VA., just south of Rockville, police have been battling violent Salvadorian gangs called MS-13. Members are illegal aliens and some have been convicted for murders in the area over the past year.

And who can forget Kathryn Steinie, 31, a medical sales rep who was strolling with her father in a tourist area, and shot randomly and killed at Pier 14 in July of 2015 in San Francisco, a sanctuary city, allegedly by Francisco Sanchez, 45, who was previously deported five times to his home country of Mexico and his criminal history includes seven prior felony convictions

None of these crimes would have occurred had immigration laws, already on the books, been upheld

Today no sense appears to prevail over common sense in the United States giving way to liberal political correctness.

Tribalism

The reptiles reared their heads from the murky DC Swamp on the 64th day of Donald J. Trump's presidency to kill his campaign promise to repeal and replace Obamacare.

Oh, it's not that they haven't surfaced before, they have on day one when a group of congressmen boycotted his inauguration, led by Rep. John Lewis, (D., GA.) civil rights icon, who said he does not regard Trump 'as a legitimate president.'

The GOP pulled the bill to repeal and replace because they couldn't get the votes from either party and they were 20 votes short in their own party.

It was a bad bill from the outset, naively prepared, rushed to get passed and didn't meet the objective of repeal and replace, for it was more like repeal and fix.

It was Trump's first defeat and sent a negative message to Wall Street, which had been doing so well. Stocks tanked as optimism diminished on the Trump agenda.

Paul Ryan, as Speaker of the House failed in his role to get the votes even if the bill was a fix rather than a replace and a first step to repair. He was out rearranging the deck chairs while the Titanic was sinking.

Nevertheless, Trump and Ryan regrouped, rather than let Obamacare implode, made modifications in the bill and it has passed the House.

Tribalism is taking hold in America because of the Trump win and the people's request for change and the call for leadership from a non-politician.

The reptiles are in the DC swamp of both parties, including the bureaucrats, whistle blowers and left-wing mainstream media.

The waves of violence across this country are being blamed on the behavior and attitudes that stem from strong loyalty to one's own tribe or social group, the definition of Tribalism.

Democrats can't talk to Republicans anymore with civility and vice versa.

Ted Koppel who is now working for CBS, and who has delivered bias reports in the form of alleged news for his entire career, told Sean Hannity, who serves up commentary, and is so identified as such for Fox News, that he was 'bad for America.'

Yet the likes of Dan Rather and Brian Williams can serve up 'fake news,' as well as bias news.

Chris Matthews, Jake Tapper, Wolf Blitzer and Matt Lauer all serve up bias reports in their news to the degree that you can't distinguish in the journalism of today the difference between news and commentary.

Dr. Tim Groseclose, who recently wrote "Left Turn," a professor of political science and economics at UCLA, has spent years constructing precise, quantitative measures of the slant of media outlets.

Among his conclusions are: (1) all mainstream media outlets have a liberal bias; and (2) while some supposedly conservative outlets – such as the Washington Times or Fox News' Special Report – do lean right, their conservative bias is less than the liberal bias of most mainstream outlets.

It was found that 18 of the top mainstream media outlets are biased toward progressive liberalism.

Wall of Opposition

President Trump was not only elected and designated as president-elect when the Democrats began building a metaphorical wall of opposition in response to his shocking win, a wall the Donald promised to physically build on the border of Mexico to help resolve the immigration problem in America.

The Dems had targets, ready to shoot at anyone that appeared vulnerable within the planned Trump administration as though they were trolling in an amusement park and came upon a shooting gallery.

It was vindictively vicious, un-American and divisively racial as former President Obama re-introduced same to the United States during his previous administration.

Bi-partisanship was not in their vocabulary, they were the leaders of the reptiles in the Swamp of DC politics.

They and their followers were not going to allow this strange, uncouth, interloper, non-politician, non-club member enter the elitists members of the austere club. He might as well could have been a black, or worse a Nazi which Trump has been called, of yesterday applying for membership in the prestigious hallow halls of the Augusta National Golf Club, where the Masters is held every year and the famous green jacket is given to the winner.

The leader of the pact of dissidents as reptiles in the DC swamp of politicians is none other than Chuck Schumer, the Dem Senator from New York, who took over the minority leadership of the Senate from Harry Reid, the Dem from Las Vegas who is still trying to learn how to stay on a treadmill.

Chuck, who is still learning how to behave in swanky New York restaurants without being rude to other customers who voted for Trump, was the Dem who said during the Bush administration, that the Senate not only has the right but the DUTY to block Supreme Court nominees from a lame-duck President.

But now with Trump in office he plans on filibustering the nomination of Neil Gorsuch to the Supreme Court, a tactic never used by the Senate in the history of the US. It didn't work. The Republicans used the nuclear option founded by former Dem Senator Harry Reid which changed the rules of filibustering Supreme Court nominees and Neil Gorsuch was confirmed Associate Supreme Court Justice.

The wall of opposition is formidable, it not only consists of Democrats in the Congress and all their supporters, there is a segment of Republicans in Congress and their supporters that are working to lay bricks on the wall and then there are the bureaucrats loyal to Obama's shadow government who are planted spy's working against the Trump presidency at least one year before it happened.

And, then the leaks are passed along to the biased liberal media for magnification.

'The last time there were leaks like this Noah built himself a boat,' an appropriate line borrowed from the movie, "Absence of Malice."

There Is no evidence of collusion within the Trump administration and Russia.

And other than WikiLeaks, and the blunders Clinton brought upon herself by not having a secure server and following State Department Rules, there is questionable evidence that Hillary Clinton's loss was influenced by anyone other than her deficient campaign performance.

Fox News reported through an anonymous source – which most of all the other sources are – that Trump was spied on before he was even nominated.

Only Fox reported this, no other news outlet within the mainstream media even referred to the report.

Tim Groseclose writes in the Preface of his book, "Left Turn", "In at least one important way journalists are very different from the rest of us – they are more liberal."

He says, according to surveys, in a typical presidential election Washington correspondents vote about 93-7 for the Democrat, while the rest of America votes about 50-50.

He asks, "What happens when our view of the world is filtered through the eyes, ears, and minds of such a liberal group?"

He goes on to point out, through objective, social-scientific methods, the filtering prevents us from seeing the world as it is.

"Instead," he says, "we see only a distorted version of it. It is as if we see the world through a glass – a glass that magnifies the facts that liberals want us to see and shrinks the facts that conservatives want us to see."

Groseclose concludes that, "The metaphoric glass affects not just what we see, but how we think. That is, media bias really does make us more liberal.

Susan Rice of Benghazi Fame Surfaces

Who would have known, Susan Rice, the woman of Benghazi fame who participated in the Obama Administration cover-up, that included presidential candidate Hillary Clinton, then Secretary of State, of the Benghazi terror attack that killed four American hero's including the Ambassador to Libya, Chris Stevens, was caused by a video tape, and said Bergdahl served with 'honor and distinction' in Afghanistan with the Army, but is now undergoing a court martial for desertion and claimed ignorance of any wiretapping of Trump by the Obama administration, turns out to be the 'deep throat' of Trump surveillance before he was ever nominated to run for the presidency of his party?

The onions growing in the swamp are being pealed back exposing the reptiles layer by layer, and so far, Trump, having served in the oval office less than 75 days, has identified the enemy. They represent the past, the present, the future, they come from within his own party, the opposition to his party, the past administration, the Democratic bureaucrats of previous administrations and the mainstream liberal media all living in the DC Swamp.

The people asked for change when they voted for Trump over Clinton, the real people, the middle class. They saw the rationale of Mark Twain's quote, "Politicians and diapers must be changed often, and for the same reason."

I like that quote, it smells somewhat of the swamp our politicians live in that obviously needs some cleansing, if not changing before the next election.

As a refresher, Susan Rice was US Ambassador to the United Nations while performing cover-up chores on Benghazi for the Obama Administration and then as an apparent pay-off, became Obama White House National Security Adviser.

As the news broke around this disclosure, Rice denied that she 'prepared' spreadsheets of surveilled telephone calls involving Donald Trump and his aides.

No news report said she 'prepared' them, they said she 'ordered' the spreadsheets to be produced.

US Attorney Joe DiGenova, one of the sources, in a response said her denial, 'would come as quite a surprise to the government officials who have reviewed dozens of those spreadsheets."

Again, the mainstream liberal media lost their pens on this story, and those that didn't, like CNN, went on a rampage against the Rice bombshell and instructed viewers to ignore the story. The National Review Summarized Rice's action well:

The national-security adviser is not an investigator. She is a White House staffer.

The president's staff gathers intelligence and is not a generator or collector of it.

According to those that have worked in these White House positions, if Susan Rice was unmasking Americans, it was not to fulfill an intelligence need; it was to fulfill a political desire based on Democratic-party interests.

Decisive

President Donald Trump took decisive, quick, targeted and strategic military action on his 77th day in office at 8:49 pm firing 60 Tomahawk missiles (could this name be politically correct?) at an airfield in Syria (4/6/17) in response to the chemical weapons attack Assad used two days before killing some 80 of his own people, including men, women, children, and babies with Sarin gas.

Trump bombed the airfield from which planes left to drop cans of Sarin gas on the people of Syria two days before. Casualties from the US airstrikes were limited, if any, while 20 Syrian planes were destroyed.

Trump sent a message not only to Syria, but to the rest of the world that the United States will act to protect its national security, unlike President Obama, a passive progressive that led from behind with threats of a red line but no follow through or action.

The decisive action also sent a message to Russia, Iran, North Korea and China, who's President, Xi Jinping, was having dinner with Trump at Mar a Lago at the very time the attack was taking place.

Earlier in the week Trump met with the Crown Prince of Saudi Arabia and the leaders of Egypt and Jordan.

If it was not clear before, Trump says what he means and means what he says and will take decisive action to support his rhetoric.

He received by-partisan support for his actions from the likes of McCain, Graham and Schumer and Pelosi.

There was world wide support from Jordan, Egypt, Saudi Arabia, led by Israel. Russia's Putin called the airstrikes 'an illegal act of aggression.' Although MSNBC host Lawrence O'Donnell thought the attack was a conspiracy between Trump and Putin.

O'Donnell theorized that Trump and Putin were in collusion on the strikes all designed to give Trump his day in the sun, a point hard-line lefties want to make that there is a conspiracy between Putin/Russia and Trump/US and they will even take it to this degree.

Meanwhile Putin sends a frigate from the Black Sea to Syria to intercept the two US destroyers that fired the missiles on a Syrian air force base and Trump sends a US Carrier strike force to the Korean Peninsula

It is an example of how fried the circuitry in the thinking process has become of the hard left since their devastating loss to Trump and how far their fantasies have parted from reality.

The action was justified, executed precisely, quickly and decisively.

And, the message went out to the world that there's a new Sheriff in town.

Invented Outrage

The hard-left prides itself in Invented Outrage, the concept for which comes from a shadow government and fed to the left-wing media as a diversion tactic from Trump's successful air strikes on Syria.

The strategy is all based upon the progressives' think tank attempting to provide a 'collusion conspiracy' between Trump and Putin on the theory, with little proof, that Russia interfered with the US presidential election providing an excuse for the Democrats humiliating loss.

Trump's successful response to Assad's human atrocities in using Sarin gas against his own men, women, children and babies, came in a surprise air attack on the very air base from which Assad's planes flew to drop the deadly gas. Some 80 persons were killed. Trump drew the red line in the sand and fulfilled a promise the previous Obama administration promised but failed to execute.

The airstrikes were executed two days after the Assad atrocities, without leaks, but with US Navy precision impressively dropping 60 Tomahawk missiles and hitting 59 targets on the airfield.

Putin called it an 'illegal act of aggression' and sent a Russian frigate to the region, Trump sent a US Carrier strike force to the Korean Peninsula.

The attack sent a message to Syria, Russia, Iran and North Korea that a new Sheriff was in town, promising more if Assad continued with his human atrocities.

Meanwhile, as the tensions mounted between Russia and the United States, the worst since the days of the 'Cold War,' the hard left continued to invent the outrage by claiming a 'collusion conspiracy' between Putin and Trump assisted in their messaging by the left-wing media delivering the 'fake news' the Donald asserts is their modus operandi.

The left invents the unbelievable, spins it to make it believable, with third party left wing media message support while the 'Snakes in the Swamp' operate as the spies from within. Sounds like a reverse form of conspiracy, doesn't it? It is!

Remember Michael Flynn, once our national security adviser and his dismissal for lying under a soft coup, or better described as a political assassination which was executed by political spies from within the swamp.

Oh, he made some mistakes, lying to the Vice President and not declaring that he was serving as an agent to Turkey. The left went after a soft Trump target trying to establish a relationship between him and Russia.

As time evolves the concept of Trump aligning himself with Putin is waning, especially since the air strikes on Syria. Nevertheless, the left is now taking the 'collusion conspiracy' to a new level of nonsense suggesting a predisposed plan involving the attack, all while Russia is aligning itself with Syria and Iran two failed countries and bringing world powers closer to war, which Russia couldn't handle and the United States doesn't want.

To think that this strategy is coming from the progressive left in the United States is un-American, un-patriotic, bizarre and ludicrous.

Surprisingly, it was the New York Times, the mouthpiece of the left, that on January 27, 2017 said, speaking of President Trump who was inaugurated on January 20th, that "No president in modern times, has started with such a flurry of initiatives on so many fronts in such short order."

The Times noted that other new occupants of the White House wanted to be judged by their first 100 days in office, President Trump, they said, seems intent to be judged by his first 100 hours.

Trump appears to have the energy of a 40-year-old, not a 70-year-old, which he is.

He also thrives on multi-tasking, while keeping in mind, his goal is to keep America first and Make America Great Again.

Within 80 days he has already improved the culture of America, created a positive attitude, which is reflected on Wall Street, received commitment from American Corporations to keep production in the United States, which means jobs, moved forward with the Keystone pipeline providing energy and jobs, moved on inter-city redevelopment, confirmed a new conservative associate Supreme Court Judge in Neil Gorsuch and improved the employment picture in the US while addressing global issues with America's Defense.

Draining the Swamp That Isn't

A widely held rumor says that Washington DC was built on a swamp. It was an early example of fake news dating back to the 1800's.

Nevertheless, if the fake news purveyors are going to report on it, Trump is going to take advantage of it. One of his campaign slogans was that he was going to 'Drain the Swamp' when he got to DC.

You see the fake swamp news has been debunked but evolved over the years as a metaphor and the Donald worked it over to his advantage as he has effectively done with fake news and the media.

Even Pierre L'Enfant, the famous French planner of DC, never noted it as being a swamp.

Bob Arnebeck who wrote an essay on, "Was Washington Built on a Swamp?" said that Boston, New York, Philadelphia and Baltimore are far better described as being built on a Swamp than Washington DC.

However, Arnebeck went on to say, "In a sense, the city became a swamp, but the swamp was and is entirely manmade. Then and now, natural advantages abound."

He must have been thinking of the Army Corps of Engineers.

So much has been exposed today as fake news, looking for the truth is like searching for a needle in a haystack.

Unfortunately, Trump couldn't get rid of all the reptiles in the metaphorical swamp in the brief time he has occupied the White House, but it appears that there are more snakes in the swamp than thought and must have been reported over the years by the same federal agency that releases the unemployment statistics.

Some snakes were planted by previous administrations others evolved over time through partisan politics and can be found in every nook and cranny feeding off any semblance of conservative thought.

When Trump launched the air strikes against Syria for human atrocities on Assad's own people he did so with some 60 Tomahawk missiles shot from two Navy destroyers.

He received bi-partisan support from within the swamp and not even a Tweet from Sen. Elizabeth Warren (D-MA.) about the political incorrectness of the missiles' name.

Apparently, Warren didn't hear one drum beat from her Native American Indian tribe, the Cherokees, from which she is an alleged descendant.

Perhaps Warren knew by reading Wikipedia, that the tomahawks were general purpose tools used by Native Americans and European colonials alike, and often employed as a hand-to-hand or a thrown weapon. The metal tomahawk heads were originally based on a Royal Navy boarding axe and used as a trade-item with Native Americans for food and other provisions.

Trump has a lot of snakes to exterminate from the metaphorical swamp called DC, and I would suggest he not ask for the Army Corps of Engineers for assistance – they did enough damage to the Florida Everglades and are still in the process of trying to put it back in the way in which they found it.

I Wouldn't Be President If It Weren't for Twitter

This is a definitive signal that President Trump is not going to be curbing his tweets, nor should he be, as they have been very effective with the media in curbing 'fake news.'

It's the first time a president has used this medium, and won't be the last.

It is another form of check and balance in our democracy, albeit of recent technology, because it precludes the media from inserting its interpretation or bias into a published statement of 140 characters from the source of the message.

President Trump said he doesn't regret sending tweets, even if some were duds.

A Tweet: 'Terrible! Just found out that Obama had my 'wires tapped' in Trump Tower just before the victory. Nothing found."

It was proven to be true without Trump offering any evidence to support the claim.

Others did such as the Benghazi truth teller Susan Rice.

"There's a lot of fake news" said Trump ... "reach 80 million people" ... "Twitter is a wonderful thing for me, because I get the word out."

Trump fired off an average of 36 tweets per week during his first 50 days in office.

The media, especially the left wing, is not happy about this development. It takes away their flexibility to possibly insert their own bias in reporting the news rather than offering their commentary, which they would have to identify.

Factual news should not contain bias, but it does by the mere nature of the way in which it is assembled.

So, there is no question that the news is slanted to the left or the right, and there is a greater likelihood today that it is preponderantly slanted to the hard left.

Let the Tweet be, it is another check and balance, but on the media.

Bombs Dropped, Messages Delivered

Tomahawk missiles on Syria, Carrier strike force to North Korea and 'Mother of all Bombs' dropped on ISIS in Afghanistan sends a powerful message from the Trump administration to Syria, Russia, Iran and North Korea about the military prowess of the United States from a leader who has established by his actions that he is not afraid to use the might at his disposal.

Unlike previous administrations, no more free lunches from the US for countries who threaten nuclear development, commit human atrocities nor enemies who attack American citizens.

Trump has drawn multiple red lines in the sand and acted upon his rhetoric.

He has demonstrated that he is not a passive progressive who leads from behind.

The bomb dropped in Afghanistan killed more than 100 members of ISIS holed up in the caves, with no civilian casualties.

It was the 13th week of the Trump administration and the bombs dropped from the skies, one from North Korea tried a launch toward the west but it hardly got off the launching pad during a celebratory weekend before it exploded, something was said about cyber interference but no country took credit for the failure – much like the Russian interference with the US elections.

Sen. Elizabeth Pocahontas Warren wanted an explanation for dropping that 'Mother of all Bombs' in Afghanistan that killed ISIS, who we are at war with. The mere fact that they are the enemy wasn't enough. I wonder if she got an explanation for her forefathers use of throwing Tomahawks at Union soldiers?

One Democratic Congressmen thought Trump's use of power during this week had to do with improving his favorability rating . . . it did reach 50%.

Unfortunately rocket scientists are not voted into leadership positions in Congress, they are more likely varmints in a swamp that can't be drained.

Whatever Happened to Yesterday . . .

Today if you voted for Trump you're a racist.

If you didn't vote for Clinton you're sexist.

And, if you like the American Flag you're political, not a patriot.

I knew my parents were Republicans, they voted for Wendel Willkie, we had Willkie buttons in our house. I never met anyone named Wendel, but I never forgot his name. He didn't win.

But my parents never talked politics, I didn't even know the difference between a Democrat and a Republican. People were just my friends.

I was shy growing up, I liked baseball and girls but my shyness didn't help with the latter. I eventually grew out of that. I was considered normal for a boy . . . I don't know what I would be considered today.

In retrospect my parents weren't wealthy, after all I was born in the depths of the Depression, and today they would have been given a cell phone by President Obama, but I'm sure they would still be Republicans.

I was seven when World War II broke out, that was a patriotic and romantic war, if a war can be called the latter.

I never saw another one that was, romantic. I know because I became an amateur historian buff of this war.

There was politics behind that war, too bad the politicians that came along thereafter failed to learn anything from it, because they continued to make the same mistakes many times thereafter with wars they tried to call something else.

I went on to college, there were no protests, the American Flag flew over our campus. There were values, students wanted to achieve, veterans came back from the war and got an education on the GI Bill.

There was freedom of speech on the campuses throughout the United States – any point of view was accepted and tolerated.

It was a time of peace, Gen. Dwight D. Eisenhower eventually became President.

Whatever happened to yesterday? I have checked my GPS and it can't take me back to those times, instead I get a fast forward to the Twilight Zone and beyond only to find protests accelerating to violence, the American Flag not flying and freedom of speech not being allowed on college campuses today.

We have come from a period where Democrats freely mingled with Republicans to a place where divisiveness prevails brought about by a previous administration's racist culture pinning blacks against whites and encouraging such groups as 'black lives matter' as though all lives don't matter.

From Notre Dame, Berkeley to Wellesley, freedom of speech is curtailed unless it contains politically correct messages from the hard left. Conservative authors and lecturers David Horowitz and Ann Coulter were both invited to speak at Berkeley and their invitations were withdrawn by the faculty for fear of violence by the students.

Security is the lefts new form of preventing the right from speaking on their campuses, because it's not safe. The speech never took place because of security reasons.

They call themselves anti-fascists, but the outcome is a fascism result with violence, campus damage, and persons injured.

Hillary Clinton, a former alumna of Wellesley, is welcomed as a commencement speaker, but Vice President Mike Pence is not at Notre Dame. It was always a tradition at Notre Dame that the new and incoming President was invited as a commencement speaker.

But this year, because of the controversy surrounding the Trump win, the invite went to Vice President Pence, but that didn't satisfy the left – a portion of them walked out before he spoke.

A few said his presence on campus would make them feel "unsafe," and others were photographed with white board quotations saying Pence was a "racist, sexist, homophobic and xenophobic."

From college campuses to Congress hate now replaces any form of respect for another point of view.

It is the direct cause of the violence we see today in the streets of America and on the elitists college campuses of America where progressive liberalism is taught without tolerance or acceptance of another point of view.

Liberal college professors have been known to teach and profess that 'it's a good thing to hate people you disagree with.'

Freedom of speech is being threatened and if that is the case so is the Constitution.

Party Above America

The Democrats are against the Wall because they want open borders to welcome new, but illegal members to their failing party. President Trump is enforcing immigration laws that are already on the books and illegal crossing have dropped 73 percent. The Dems are in favor of the 'catch and release' policy of Obama.

Dems are against anything Trump is for, such as jobs, an improved healthcare system rather than Obamacare, a sound economy, keeping manufacturing in America, a strong military, and freedom of speech.

Democrats place Party above the United States, when they deliver a message you can't find what they are for, but you can tell what they are against for most of the rhetoric is anti-Trump filled with obscene redacted language.

It is how Hillary Clinton lost the presidential election to Trump, no one knew what she was for, only what she was against – Trump – not realizing what he was saying was resonating with the people.

Take, for example. Democratic National Committee Chairman, Tom Perz comments on a Democratic 'unity' tour, proclaiming that Trump "doesn't give a shit about people or their health care." Perez even noted at a Vegas speech that his mother told him not to use 'potty' language and then proceeded to call Trump's financial agenda a "shitty budget," all of this foul language was taking place as a young child was no more than a few feet from Perez' podium.

On college campuses across the United States violence is promoted by encouraging left-wing snowflakes to mute free speech.

Hate and violence appear to be a credo of Democrats, if one utters what they oppose hate them; if they pursue their thesis, create violence. The Party even holds seminars for the snowflakes on how not to and how to safely get arrested.

The 100th Day

While the media was patting itself on the back in Washington DC at the White House Correspondents' dinner for not printing 'fake news,' 100 miles away in Harrisburg, Pa. President Trump was ripping them apart for doing the very thing they say they don't do at a rally drawing 11,000 supporters.

Reporters bristled while clinking wine glasses when they heard the president say to his audience "I could not possibly be more thrilled than to be more than 100 miles away from the Washington swamp spending my evening with all of you and with a much larger crowd and much better people."

Trump decided in February to boycott the star-studded tinseled affair held annually in April for a rally in Harrisburg on his 100th day in office.

However, it didn't stop his bashing of the press. He slammed reporters as "incompetent, dishonest people." He said they too "should be judged" for their performance in the past 100 days. He went on to say, "If the media's job is to be honest and tell the truth, then I think we would all agree the media deserves a very, very big fat failing grade."

Back in Washington the media whined, "we are not fake news, we are not failing news organizations and we are not the enemy of the American people," Reuter's Jeff Mason said in an address to the gathering as president of the WHCA.

Nevertheless, the Snakes in the Swamp who hate Trump and he may not be counting them in his Crocodile Dundee walk-about in the DC Swamp, including some members of Congress, imbedded bureaucrats in the government, the Democrat Party and their constituents, leftover spies from the Obama Administration, the voting liberals who after 100 days were just getting out of bed after Hillary Clinton's loss, some of whom will never get over it, as Trump began telling his audience what he accomplished in his first 100 days.

He talked about immigration and how he reduced illegal immigrants by 73 percent from crossing our border by enforcing existing laws and without a wall, but still feels the wall is necessary.

He then went on to explain a poem that was written that he equates to illegal immigrants, a metaphor, if you will. It was written by Al Wilson in 1968:

The Snake

On her way to work one morning
Down the path alongside the lake
A tender-hearted woman saw a poor half frozen snake

His pretty colored skin had been all frosted with the dew

"Poor thing," she cried, "I'll take you in and I'll take care of you"

"Take me in tender woman

Take me in, for heaven's sake

Take me in, tender woman," sighed the snake

She wrapped him all cozy in a comforter of silk

And laid him by her fireside with some honey and some milk

She hurried home from work that night and soon as she arrived

She found that pretty snake she'd taken to had been revived

"Take me in, tender woman

Take me in, for heaven's sake

Take me in, for heaven's sake

Take me in, tender woman," sighed the snake

She clutched him to her bosom, "You're so beautiful," she cried

"But If I hadn't brought you in by now you might have died"

She stroked his pretty skin again and kissed and held him tight

Instead of saying thanks, the snake gave her a vicious bite

"Take me in, tender woman

Take me in, for heaven's sake

Take me in, woman," sighed the snake

"I saved you," cried the woman
"And you've bitten me, but why?
You know your bite is poisonous and
now I'm going to die"
"Oh shut up, silly woman," said the
reptile with a grin
"You knew damn well I was a snake
before you took me in
"Take me in, tender woman
Take me in, for heaven's sake
Take me in, tender woman," sighed the
snake.

And so, the lesson learned is that there
are more snakes in the DC swamp than those
that are identified as being illegal immigrants.

After Trump refused the correspondents
dinner invite his staff also boycotted the
dinner in solidarity.

The organizers of the dinner invited
Woodward and Bernstein of Watergate fame,
who buttressed the cause of the journalists, and
the Association asked their emcee, "Daily
Show" comedian Hasan Minhaj not to make
fun of Trump.

Minhaj ignored the request, broiled
Trump and defended free speech.

He said, "Only in America can a first-generation Indian-American Muslim kid get on this stage and make fun of the president, the orange man behind the Muslim ban," he said. "This shows the entire world that even the president is not beyond the reach of the first amendment."

But all this narrative did not end in DC, Trump apparently realized illegal aliens were not the only threats to his presidency, for he then launched an attack on Senate Minority leader Charles Schumer (D-NY):

"Sen. Schumer is a bad leader, not a natural leader at all," Trump said. "He works hard to study leadership. When you have to study leadership, you've got problems."

"Schumer is weak on crime and wants to raise your taxes through the roof," Trump continued. "He is a poor leader, known him a long time, and he's leading the Democrats to doom. It's sad to see for our country, what's happening to the Democrat Party."

And so, we can be assured that Trump realizes there are other forms of reptiles in the swamp in which he is required to operate.

Epilogue

The first 100 days are over. What was learned? There are more snakes in the DC swamp than anyone thought. Draining it should be a line item in the budget for all future presidents, unless he himself is one of them; under that situation the purpose of draining the swamp would be redundant, as was demonstrated in the past eight years of the Obama administration.

When President Trump ran for the nomination, subsequently winning and came into the oval office, he was an outsider, a non-politician or political elitist. He may have been an elitist in the world of wealth but certainly not in the world of politics.

In fact, his own Republican Party didn't want him as a candidate, the elitists within his party were opposed to his run as were the 16 other candidates that he eviscerated.

There were leaders like Paul Ryan, John McCain and Lindsey Graham, who formed their own club and were more like the Dems then members of the GOP.

To say that Trump was not welcome in the Oval Office or among the elitists in DC would be an understatement.

Since he took office, a new paradigm was nosily exposed among the sore losers, it was complex, unacceptable behavior with protests that took place in violence, meanwhile the right was growing into a silent majority supporting the change they brought to America in the name of President Trump.

It was he that found them, not them that found him, with a Tweet, a business acumen, anything but a style of a politician and promises that one could believe in after seeing the world-wind actions of the first 100 days.

Here are some of the accomplishments:

- Building American prosperity
- Over 500,000 new jobs
- Dakota Acers pipeline and Keystone SL pipeline
- America's energy independence
- Rolled back job-killing anti coal regulations
- Buy American hire American
- American worker first
- Illegal border crossings dropped
- Holding sanctuary cities accountable
- Action against Syria to combat use of chemical weapons
- New sanctions on Iran

- Boosting military strength, empowering military
- Increased national security budget
- Agency reorganization
- Launched Opioid abuse commission
- Lobbying ban
- Improved veterans care
- Nominated and confirmed Justice Neil Gorsuch to Supreme Court

Not all the promises were there to make you a believer, but enough were to set a tone that was positive, a culture that was conducive to business, jobs, and an environment that was favorable to the stock market.

These were positive intangibles while the left delivered negative protests, violence and hate in the streets of America.

Barbara Streisand was crying rather than singing, Stephen Colbert was crude, vulgar and mindlessly sick in his monologue rather than funny and Bill Mahar was gross and crass, more so than usual, trying to keep up with Colbert.

Meanwhile Hillary Clinton said in an interview on CNN that she would be president if it were not for James Comey of the FBI, Putin of Russia and WikiLeaks distributing her emails that came off her illegal server which was hiding in the bathroom of her home.

The first 100 days of the Trump administration moved at such a fast pace, accomplishing promised campaign pledges, the mouths of the left wing progressive liberals, including the snakes in Congress, were choking on their own venom.

And, hypocrisy was given a bad name when President Trump fired James Comey, Director of the FBI. There were 20 Democrats and Republicans at one point or another who called for the firing of James Comey over his actions during the investigation of Hillary Clinton's hacked emails, when she was still a candidate for president.

The timing for the firing some said was wrong, it came when the FBI was considering some form of collusion that was allegedly, according to the Dems, taking place between Russia and the Trump campaign to influence the US elections.

Trump fires him and the Congressional Democrats along with a smattering of Republican elitists, now call it a Trump cover-up for an unproven charge of collusion with Russia; it is a charge the snakes think is better than all the other flak because it can always be charged, if never proven to be true.

The collusion that really takes place is that between the Democrats and the left-wing mainstream progressive media, that now goes far beyond the New York Times and the Washington Post serving as a part-time mouthpiece, proliferating fake news for the hard left rather than journalism for the people.

The hard left is now calling for an investigation in search of a crime. It is not enough that four federal agencies have launched investigations into an alleged charge of collusion between Trump and all the president's men and found nothing in nine months. The Dems want an independent prosecutor to be named to further investigate it, at least, until the end of Trump's first term in office.

Obstruction, deflection, deception, protests, violence, arrests, black lives matter, divisiveness, racism, sexism, homophobe and Islamophobia are stigmatizing words and tactics used by progressives that follow in the teachings of Saul Alinsky and his model for radicals.

It was cemented in the foundation President Obama attempted to build during the past eight years of his administration to be, 'willing to destroy the values, structures and institutions that sustain the society in which we live' and rejected in the election of President Trump.

However, Obama built up a hatred within the Democratic Party that has now taken America to a place where liberal journalism is a blood sport.

The Dems got what they wanted a special prosecutor was named, former FBI Director Robert Mueller, with whom Comey had previously worked. There was no resistance from the Republican leadership and the likes of Ryan, McCain or Graham.

Former Harvard Professor of Law and Civil Libertarian Alan Dershowitz, a Democrat who voted for Clinton, calls the naming of a Special Prosecutor 'the road to Stalinism.'

He said the firing of Comey was appropriate and Trump had every right to do it. Furthermore, he said it is, "unlikely that any federal crimes were committed." He also said the appointing of a special counsel with the Justice Department is not to learn the whole truth. He went on to say, "The role of a special counsel, like every prosecutor, is adversarial. Neither a criminal investigation nor a criminal trial is a search for truth."

The Swamp is awash in quicksand, the leaks within the White House and the Intel community make it appear as a fourth branch of government formed to govern with undercover agents funneling negative conservative info onto their partners in crime the left-wing media who are now practicing their blood sport called journalism in behalf of Democrats who are spreading hatred among America.

Bringing down a presidency for lack of cause, least of all a crime, does not represent a democracy, it is what President Trump labeled it, "A Witch Hunt."

Today, Democrats do not represent a democracy, they represent hatred, violence, protests and least of all freedom of speech, except for a few like Alan Dershowitz an extraordinary attorney, Democrat and civil libertarian.

I was personally struck by the juxtaposition of two comments made at a commencement address, one by a Democrat, the other by a Republican. It tells a story of leadership in America today:

Rep. John Lewis (D-Ga), a civil rights icon, in addressing the graduating students at the Massachusetts College of Liberal Arts, called on students to "get in the way" and "get in trouble" because the "country needs you now more than ever before." Was he really talking about Country, or was it "Party?"

Meanwhile President Trump speaking at commencement ceremonies at Liberty University said: "In America we don't worship government, we worship God."

I will leave it to the 'silent majority' to judge the appropriate leadership for the country. I personally trust the judgment of the people as was expressed in the last election.

~

Politicians excel in not telling the truth, it's in their genes.

There is no fake news, there is only false news.

In 100 days, the Donald found there were snakes in the swamp he wanted to drain.

He never envisioned himself as Crocodile Dundee with a knife, in a swamp that was not drainable.

Nor did he think the media was trolling the swamp for leakers who were liberal progressives in collusion with Democrats and Republicans who wanted to overthrow his presidency, much like the Russians.

After 100 days, the Donald took a nine-day trip throughout the Mideast and Europe demonstrating that he could excel in diplomacy like few before him.

He, his family and staff hit homeruns each stop along the way, by his own assessment, supportive pundits and myself.

However, the liberal media only saw and reported Melania slapping the Donald's hand away a hand he wanted to hold, shoving the PM of Montenegro aside to be in the front row for a photo op, and leaks coming from back home in the quicksand of the DC swamp talking about a connection with Russia and the Trumps, a throwback to the McCarthyism era of the 50's.

The loser in more ways than one, along with ISIS, labeled by the Donald, was Hillary Clinton.

She tried to draw a straight line between Trump and Nixon saying the latter president was charged with obstruction of justice and impeached. She was wrong. Nixon wasn't impeached, he resigned.

It was her husband, Bill Clinton, who was the second president who was ever impeached for perjury.

More fake news that was false.

The Donald came home in his Crocodile Dundee outfit ready to deal with the swamp - well not exactly - holding Melania's hand – exactly.

Postscript

If the Donald expected a welcome to DC after defeating Hillary Clinton for the presidency and all the other GOP elitists he was sorely mistaken.

From the outset, it was more like being led to the edge of the swamp, introduced to the quicksand, followed by the snakes, crocodiles, vultures, moles and varmints.

It was a time to take off the blue suit and red tie and don the croc hat, snake vest and pants, draw the Bowie knife from its holster ready for use.

While his supporters turned out for his inaugural speech, parade and celebratory balls, they eventually went home and left Trump to deal with the snakes in the Swamp who were vindictive enough to boycott the celebration for a day preparing for protests, obstruction and the undermining of a presidency.

Thereafter no one associated with Trump, supporters, family or even one wearing a red hat went unscathed from attack or even violence.

Protests went to violence, segued to hatred and invaded families.

Trump was jealously disliked as a successful billionaire developer before becoming a candidate, once a maverick candidate that wiped out a GOP field of elitists from within his own party, the hatred grew and then the ultimate insult, he defeated the Democratic 'entitled' elitist candidate for the presidency and he became a target for impeachment by all the Snakes from within the swamp.

The act of Impeachment is not a legal act, but a political one from the snakes and moles left behind by Obama's shadow government and within Trump's own party.

This statement is not fake news – it is factual.

And there is nothing that demonstrates this thesis more than the testimony of fired James Comey, the self-admitted 'cowardly' left-over Hoover-like Director of the Federal Bureau of Matters, (FBM).

No FBM is not a typo, that's what happened when Loretta Lynch, former Attorney General, told Comey during the Hillary email investigation to roll over like an obedient dog and call that FBI investigation a 'Matter' so it would fit with the rhetoric Hillary was delivering during her presidential campaign.

Coincidentally this occurred after Bill, Hillary's husband of presidential past tense, met with Lynch in a plane on the tarmac of the Arizona Airport.

Comey, held a press conference on the Clinton emails, delivered a virtual indictment of Hillary's handling of her emails on a private server, but declared there was no intent and exonerated her.

Balderdash!

But with Trump, who Comey was testifying about before a Senate Sub Committee, he said he didn't want to create "a J. Edgar Hoover situation," which is precisely what he did.

He then went on to tell that during his meetings with Trump, who he didn't trust, he made extensive notes. He held them secretly in fear of losing his job.

The notes he made were not made at the time of the meetings, but perhaps hours later, which become very questionable whatever grades Comey got in his higher education as to how accurate they might be.

He then passes them along to the New York Times through a trusted third party. No wonder the Times is having trouble with fake news.

He testified, after he was fired, that he gave those notes to a Professor at Columbia to leak to the New York Times.

And so, the Director of the FBI is now a whistleblower, a questionable act where some are lauded and others are convicted for being a traitor.

He admitted to this act in his testimony and did it with previous administrations in which he served.

The progressive left, with the help of the Democratic Senators and some Republicans who are out to get Trump, believe he gave a credible performance.

He has been portrayed as a Boy Scout, I certainly, hope he was not an Eagle Scout, or here goes the reputation of another institution – how about settling for a 'leaker,' a 'whistleblower,' or 'mentor of J. Edgar Hoover?

This might be more of an accurate description of his performance. The circus leading up to the Comey testimony was somewhat of a fading three ring performance, as is the case with circuses of today. Bars opened early with wide screen TV's not tuned into sporting events, but the Comey Senate hearing.

One pub offered free drinks every time Trump Tweeted during the hearing but none were served. Comey, unwittingly, did four favors for Trump. He revealed that he was not under investigation for collusion with the

Russians involving the election, that there was no evidence of collusion with the Russians at this point, that Loretta Lynch, former Attorney General asked him to change the word investigation of Hillary's emails to 'matters' so it would coincide with her campaign rhetoric – a possible obstruction of justice – and he complied, with that and he (Comey) admitted he was a 'leaker.

The columnist Michael Goodwin of the New York Post strung together the Comey timeline based upon his testimony, compared it with news events and suggests that Comey possibly made more than one leak to the media.

He says, "Comey reveals himself to be a fellow traveler with Never Trumpers. His firing brought him out of the shadows and into the open 'resistance' to the president."

Goodwin's sleuthing with Comey's help uncovered:

Comey admitted to the Senate he leaked just one memo criticizing Trump over the Gen. Michael Flynn case, asking a friend to give it to The New York Times. In its May 16 story, the paper identified its sources only as "two people who read the memo."

"But that was not the first leak," says Goodwin, "for the Times had reported five days earlier on a separate, personal Comey memo attacking Trump for demanding 'loyalty,' calling its anonymous sources" Mr Comey's associates."

Then Goodwin says, Wait, that wasn't the first leak, either. On March 5, one day after Trump accused President Barack Obama of wiretapping him at Trump Tower, the Times reported that Comey was furious at the charge. Its unnamed sources were "senior American officials."

All three stories carried the byline of Michael Schmidt, as did others that described intimate details of Comey's dealings with Trump. "Clearly," says Goodwin, "Schmidt had very, good sources close to Comey."

I believe Trump is the right man to be president for today's times and so do the people, despite what has turned into, brainwashing by design, throughout our educational system and a campaign of 'resistance,' violence and hatred by progressive elitist naysayers.

Stay the course, Mr. President, and remember:

~

"Well Begun is half Done"
Aristotle

~

Acknowledgment

I would like to express my appreciation to Michael White, the illustrator extraordinaire, from Sarasota, Florida for capturing on the cover of this book in art what I was saying in words. And, for highlighting my bushy eyebrows and making them into an interesting caricature which I also use on my website, https://donstorch.com

About the Author

During his career, Don Storch has been a journalist, editor, corporate public relations executive and crisis and issue management consultant.

He currently is a conservative columnist and author writing for the website DonStorch.com home of the Storch Report.

He is a graduate of Fairleigh Dickinson University.

He and his wife live on Manasota Key, a barrier reef on the Southwest Coast of Florida.

"Snakes in the Swamp"

'Snakes in the Swamp' come in the form of bureaucrats, Republicans, Democrats, spies in the form of the FBI, CIA, NSA, lobbyists, consultants, friends, politicians – who make for strange bedfellows – and any other varmint living within the metropolitan radius of Washington DC., such as the Media. Not all are reptiles, but there are enough from within to turn a non-politician, businessman into 'Crocodile Dundee.'

A concise, insightful commentary on Donald J. Trump's first 100 days as President of the United States. Storch has nailed this period with precision, highlighting events and Trump's accomplishments despite the backlash from the opposition, as well as from his own party. Told in a unique style, Storch explores the bold moves as Trump forges ahead, regardless of the negative press, vowing to keep the promises he has made to the country he loves.

No fake news here, this is the real thing . . . read on

www.ingramcontent.com/pod-product-compliance
Lightning Source LLC
Chambersburg PA
CBHW062014280526
45787CB00005B/2102